Living in
ENGLAND

Annabelle Lynch

W

FRANKLIN WATTS
LONDON • SYDNEY

First published in 2014 by
Franklin Watts
338 Euston Road
London
NW1 3BH

Franklin Watts Australia
Level 17/207 Kent Street
Sydney
NSW 2000

HB ISBN 978 1 4451 2793 4
Library ebook ISBN 978 1 4451 2797 2

Dewey number: 942'.08612
A CIP catalogue record for this book is
available from the British Library.

Series Editor: Julia Bird
Series Design: D.R. ink

Picture credits: Steve Allen/Dreamstime: 18b. Noam Armonn/Shutterstock: 17b. Aleksander Bedrin/Dreamstime: 4t.
Bikeworldtravel/Shutterstock: 11c, 11b, 21t. Dan Breckwoldt/Shutterstock: 9b. c byatt-norman/Shutterstock: 15t.
Colouria Media Ltd/Alamy: 19b. David Crosby/Shutterstock: 7b. Stephen Dorey /Alamy: 21b.
Kevin Eaves/Shutterstock: 13t. eye35/Alamy: 9t. Eddy Galeotti/Shutterstock: 11t. JM Gelpi/Shutterstock: 18t.
Tatiana Gladskikh/Shutterstock: front cover tcr. gorillaimages/Shutterstock: 16t. Alison Henley/Shutterstock: 17t.
Vojta Herout/Shutterstock: 7c. Adrian Hughes/Shutterstock: 16b. Pawel Kowalczyk/Shutterstock: 10b.
Nolte Lourens/Shuttertock: 8t. Phiip Minnis/istockphoto: 19t. Monkey Business Images/Shutterstock: 14t.
Mr Pics/Shutterstock: 12b. Olga Nayashkova/Shutterstock: 14b. Sergey Novikov/Shutterstock: front cover tl.
Olgysha/Shutterstock: 12t. Pavel L Photo/Shutterstock: 20t. photofriday/Shutterstock: 8b.
pio3/Shutterstock: front cover. © Robert Harding Picture Library Ltd/Alamy: 20b. tcl.
2xSamara.com/Shutterstock: front cover tr. Samot/Shutterstock: front cover b.
Adrian Sherratt/Alamy: 6b. Shestakoff/Shutterstock: front cover tlc. Alexander Trinitatov/Shutterstock: 6t.
Tupungato/Shutterstock: 5b. Ian Thwaites/Shutterstock: 13b. Jaren Wicklund/Dreamstime: 10t. Jim Wileman/Alamy: 15b.
witchcraft/Shutterstock: 5t. Zurijeta/Shutterstock: front cover trc.

Printed in China

Franklin Watts is a division of
Hachette Children's Books,
an Hachette UK company.
www.hachette.co.uk

Contents

Words in bold are in the glossary on page 23.

Welcome to England

Hello! I come from England. It is one of the four countries of the United Kingdom.

England in the UK

England is the biggest country in the UK. It shares a **border** with Scotland in the north and Wales in the west.

N
W E
S

Lake District

Yorkshire Dales

Pennines

Blackpool

Liverpool

Manchester

Birmingham

ENGLAND

LONDON

Stonehenge

South Downs

St Ives

Brighton

Isle of Wight

English Channel

SCOTLAND

NORTHERN IRELAND

ENGLAND

WALES

Hills and mountains

England is mostly flat, with some gentle, rolling hills. In the north and west there are some bigger hills and mountains. The Pennine hills run through the middle of the north of the country.

Rain or shine?

The weather in England can be different every day! Usually, we have warm summers and mild winters, although it does snow sometimes. Rain can fall at any time in the year.

People in England

I come from England. People who come from England are called English.

Busy place

Around 53 million people live in England. It has the biggest **population** of all of the countries in the United Kingdom. Over the years, people have come to live in England from countries all over the world, including China, India and the West Indies.

Religions

Some people brought their religion with them when they came to live in England. Around half of people are Christian. There are also lots of Muslims and Hindus. Many people don't follow any religion.

Hindu temple →

Where people live

Most people in England live close to a city, where they can find work. Lots of people live in the south-east, near London. Fewer people live in the countryside.

Religion in England
....
Christian: 31.5 million
Muslim: 2.6 million
Hindu: 800,000
No religion: 13 million

English villages are often built around a church.

Cities

There are lots of cities in England and they are all different. I live in the city of Liverpool, in north-west England.

Mersey magic

Liverpool lies on the River Mersey, next to the Irish Sea. It is an important **port.** Ships set sail from here carrying **goods** all over the world. Liverpool is also famous for its music and its football team!

Liverpool Football Club is over a hundred years old.

Birmingham

Birmingham is the second biggest city in the UK, after London (see pages 10–11). It is in the centre of England. There used to be lots of **factories** here. Today, many people go to Birmingham to work, see music or art shows, or shop.

Biggest cities
....

London: 8 million
Birmingham: 2.3 million
Manchester: 1.7 million

Seaside fun

Brighton is one of the smaller cities in England. It is on the south **coast**. It has a big pebbly beach and a long **pier**. Lots of people visit Brighton for a fun day by the sea!

London

*I live in London. It is the **capital** city of England and the biggest city in the UK. Around eight million people live here!*

Early days

London is in the south-east corner of England. People have lived here for over two thousand years. Some still use the River Thames, which runs through London, for **transport**.

Thirlmere in the Lake District.

Countryside

England has big parks where the countryside is protected. Some of the most famous are the Lake District, the Yorkshire Dales and the South Downs. People visit them to go walking and hiking.

Grey seals on a Norfolk beach.

Wildlife

Lots of sea birds fly above England's coast. Seals, dolphins and many kinds of fish swim in the sea. In the countryside you can see wild ponies, otters and lots of other animals.

What we eat

There are lots of different foods to try in England. Some of them are found all over the UK. Others are special to England.

Breakfast time

You can start the day with an English breakfast. This usually has bacon, eggs, sausages, mushrooms, tomatoes, baked beans and toast. Most people just have toast or a bowl of cereal though.

Sunday roast

At weekends, people often get together for a roast dinner. There is a big piece of meat such as beef or lamb, roast potatoes and gravy, vegetables and sometimes a dish called Yorkshire pudding.

Time for tea?

Sandwiches are named after an English man called the Earl of Sandwich. He ate them while he played cards!

Take-away?

Fish and chips is one of the most popular take-aways. People traditionally ate them wrapped in newspaper. Today, you can get take-away meals from all over the world in England, including Chinese stir-fries, Indian curries and Turkish **kebabs**.

Having fun

There are many different ways to have fun in England! We love being outdoors when the Sun shines. We also love playing and watching sport.

Out and about

In summer, we go cycling and hiking. We also head to the seaside to swim, fish, surf or just enjoy the sunshine. St Ives and Blackpool are two popular seaside towns.

The beautiful beach at St Ives.

Sports fans

Football is England's most popular sport and people all over the world watch the Premier League. Rugby and cricket also have lots of fans. Every summer, the top tennis players play at Wimbledon, near London.

Wimbledon is a famous tennis competition.

At home

When it's raining, there are still plenty of things to do. People visit family and friends, go shopping or visit the cinema. Or they watch TV or play games on the computer at home!

Famous places

England has lots of great places to visit, both old and new.

Tower of London

In London you can visit the Tower of London. People who made the king or queen angry used to be kept here. The famous **crown jewels** are also kept here.

Spooky place

They say that ghosts walk around the Tower of London at night, but it probably isn't true!

Old stones

On Salisbury Plain, you can see Stonehenge.
It is a circle of huge stones that has been there
for over 5,000 years, but nobody really knows for
sure how or why it was built.

Eating out

One yummy place to visit
in Birmingham is Cadbury
World. The famous
chocolate is made here.
You can help to make it,
go on rides and eat some
delicious chocolate!

Festivals & special days

We celebrate lots of the same festivals in England as all over the world, such as Christmas and Diwali. Some are special to England though.

Remember, remember!
The fifth of November,
The gunpowder treason and plot;
I know of no reason
Why the gunpowder treason
Should ever be forgot!

Fiery festival

On 5 November, we remember a man called Guy Fawkes who tried to blow up the English **Parliament** over 400 years ago. We light bonfires and let off fireworks.

Party time

Every summer the Notting Hill Carnival celebrates West Indian music, dance and food. People from all over the country come to have a good time!

→

Cheese-rolling

Every spring in a place called Cooper's Hill, a very funny festival takes place. People run down a very steep hill, chasing a big round cheese! The winner gets to take the cheese home.

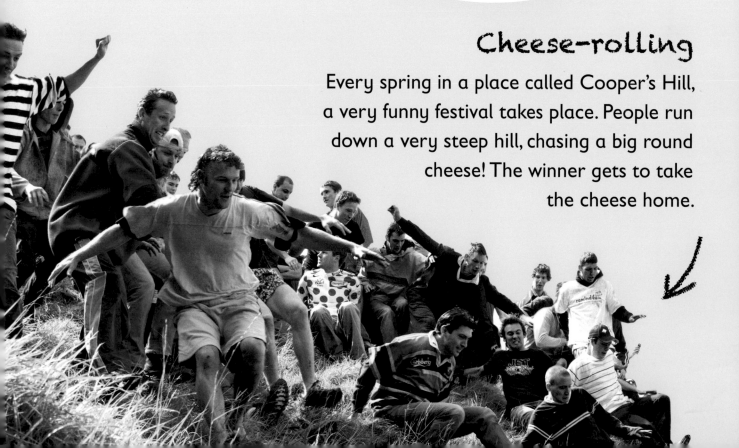

England: Fast facts

Capital: London

Population: 53 million (2011)

Area: 130,395 square km

Official language: English

Currency: Pound sterling

Main religions: Christianity, Islam, Hinduism

Longest river: River Thames (346 km)

Highest mountain: Scafell Pike

National holidays:
New Year's Day (1 January),
Good Friday, Easter Sunday,
first Monday in May, last Monday
in May, last Monday in August,
Christmas Day (25 December),
Boxing Day (26 December)

Glossary

border a line that divides two countries

capital the city in which the government of a country meets

cliff a steep, rocky hill, usually by the sea

coast where the land meets the sea

construction building work

crown jewels jewels and precious objects that belong to the king or queen. They include crowns, swords, rings and robes

factories places where lots of things are made

goods things that people can buy or sell

kebab pieces of meat which are cooked on a stick

Parliament the group of people who decide or change the laws of a country

pier a walkway out into the sea

population the number of people living in a place

port a place by the sea from where boats and ships arrive and depart

route the way from one place to another

transport a way of getting from one place to another, such as by car, bus or aeroplane

24

Index